KNOW ABOUT

Things with Wings

Big Birds

Little Birds

Eyes on the Prize

Rainbow of Colors

Weird and Wonderful

Flightless Birds

Flying Bugs

D1665738

Big Birds

There are about 10,000 different kinds of birds. Birds flap their wings up and down to fly. They also spread them out wide to glide.

Terror birds lived 65 million to 2 million years ago. They could not fly, but they stood up to 10 feet (3 meters) tall.

Wandering albatrosses are the largest seabirds. They have a wingspan of more than 10 feet (3 meters). They can glide for hours without flapping their wings.

Giant petrels live in Antarctica. On land, they can kill other large birds, such as king penguins.

Birds have light **skeletons**. Most of their bones are hollow to help them fly.

A bird's **chest muscles**, or pectorals, are its largest muscles. They lift and pull down the wings during flight.

Goliath herons are the world's largest herons. They stand about 5 feet (1.5 meters) tall. They use their long beak to spear fish, frogs, and snakes.

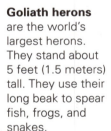

Cormorants live along freshwater and saltwater shores. They often hold out their wings to dry.

Pelicans have a long bill with a large pouch. They can sit on the water and scoop up fish.

Storks fly with their long neck outstretched. They have no vocal organs, so they communicate by clapping their bills.

Little Birds

Small birds can easily hide their nests in trees, woods, caves, and barns.
Small birds have strong muscles to flap their wings.

Hummingbirds hover in the air by rapidly flapping their wings. The bee hummingbird is the smallest bird in the world. They can fly backward too. Hummingbirds feed on the nectar of flowers.

Barn swallows usually nest in barns and caves or under bridges. They make nests from mud and grass.

Swifts are fast, high-flying birds. They often swoop in groups. Like swallows, they have forked tails.

Eurasian nuthatches are named for their ability to crack open nuts with their strong bill. They can climb down trees easily using their sharp claws.

Adult birds swallow their food, then bring up the half-digested food for their chicks. This is called regurgitation. **American robins** eat beetles, caterpillars, and fruit.

Male **scarlet tanagers** are bright red during summer. Then they shed their feathers, or molt, and become green during winter.

The color of **blue jays** makes them easily recognizable. They also make a variety of loud calls to scare off predators, such as hawks.

When a **Eurasian bullfinch** hatches, its eyes are closed and it has no feathers. ➡

After six days, its eyes are open. ➡

At 28 days, feathers start to grow along its wings. ➡

At nine months, a bullfinch is fully grown. It is about 6 inches (15 centimeters) in length.

Eyes on the Prize

Many birds eat fruit, seeds, nuts, or insects. Some birds hunt other birds and small animals for food. They are called birds of prey or raptors. Birds of prey have large, sharp claws and are expert flyers.

Ospreys eat mainly fish. As they fly over water, they can hook fish with their curved claws. They also have barbed pads on the soles of their feet.

Harpy eagles are strong enough to kill monkeys, lizards, sloths, and opossums. They can grab their prey with their claws and drag it out of a tree.

Secretary birds have the longest legs of any raptor. They kill small animals by stomping on them!

Andean condors are a kind of vulture. Their wingspan can reach 10 feet (3 meters). This bird scavenges for food from dead animals, such as sheep and llamas.

Pygmy falcons may be the smallest raptor, but they can catch large insects and small lizards. They swoop down quickly to surprise their prey.

Owls hunt at night. They glide down silently to sneak up on their prey. Owls eat rodents, insects, birds, and frogs.

Snail kites have specially curved beaks to pull out apple snails from their shell. They live in marshes and swamps.

Not all flying animals are birds. **Bats** are the only mammals that can fly. They hang upside down when they rest. Some bats eat fruits, while others eat insects.

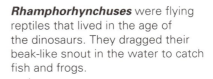

Rhamphorhynchuses were flying reptiles that lived in the age of the dinosaurs. They dragged their beak-like snout in the water to catch fish and frogs.

Terror bird

Wandering albatross

Chest muscles

Goliath heron

Stork

Scarlet tanager

Pelican

Giant petrel

Hummingbird

Skeleton

Eurasian bullfinch
hatching

Barn swallow

Eurasian Nuthatch

American robins

Cormorant

Swifts

Eurasian bullfinch at six days

Eurasian bullfinch at 28 days

Eurasian bullfinch at nine months

Blue jay

Secretary bird

Harpy eagle

Owls

Osprey

Scarlet minivets

Pygmy falcon

Rhamphorhynchus

Bat

Andean condors

Eastern rosella

Snail kite

Scarlet macaw

Blue-footed booby

Great blue turaco

Scarlet ibis

Malachite kingfisher

Bird of paradise

Frigatebird

Roseate spoonbill

Resplendent
quetzals

Toucan

Flamingos

Puffin

Pterodaustro

Shoebill

Satin bowerbird

Indian peacock

Fairy penguin

Emperor penguin

Emu egg

Ostrich

Grebes

Emus

Rhea

Kiwi

Moth

Kakapo

Butterfly

Ladybug

Cicada

Butterfly wings

Honeybee

Lacewing

Grasshopper

Dragonfly

Rainbow of Colors

Some birds have bright feathers, or plumage. Male birds are often particularly colorful in order to attract a female. Multicolored plumage helps some birds hide in their colorful surroundings.

Parrots are well known for their bright plumage. **Scarlet macaws** used to be popular as pets; they are now an endangered species.

Australia has many kinds of parrots. **Eastern rosellas** are very intelligent. They can be trained to whistle and learn words.

Resplendent quetzal feathers were prized by the ancient peoples of Central and South America. Male birds have a yellow crest and long, green tail feathers.

Male **birds of paradise** call loudly, dance, and shake their feathers to attract a female. This bird of paradise is the national bird of Papua New Guinea.

Scarlet minivets are small birds that rest while they are flying. They save energy by tucking in their wings on the downward stroke.

Malachite kingfishers have metallic blue feathers. Young birds have black bills. Their bill turns orange as they grow older.

Boobies are seabirds that are related to gannets. **Blue-footed boobies** attract females with their bright blue feet.

Scarlet ibises get darker as they grow older. They get their reddish color from the pigments in the shrimp and crabs that they eat.

Great blue turacos come from West Africa. The red tip on their beak looks as if they are wearing lipstick!

Weird and Wonderful

Birds come in many shapes and sizes. Their beak and feet are specially suited to catching certain foods. Birds also use these parts to defend themselves.

Shoebills stand more than 3 feet (1 meter) tall. Their shoe-shaped bill has a hook to help them catch lungfish, their favorite food.

Roseate spoonbills wade in shallow water. They swing their bill from side to side to look for fish and frogs.

Flamingos have long, flexible necks to reach the water. Their bill is used upside down and can filter shrimp and algae from mud and water.

Male **frigatebirds** have a huge, red throat sac. They inflate it in order to attract a female.

Indian peacocks fan out their tail to attract peahens. The tails can have up to 200 vivid blue-green feathers. They can reach 5 feet (1.5 meters) in length.

Puffins can hold about 10 fish at a time in their large, triangular bill. Their bill loses its color after the breeding season.

Toucans are well-known rainforest birds. Their large bill is hollow and light, with saw-like edges. Their call sounds like a croaking frog.

Male **satin bowerbirds** make structures called bowers, filled with stones, shells, berries, flowers, even plastic or glass items, that are mainly blue in color.

Pterodaustros were flying reptiles with bristles on their jaw. The bristles were used to filter algae and tiny marine animals from the water.

Flightless Birds

All birds have wings, although some cannot fly. These flightless birds have developed their own ways to move around, catch food, and escape from predators.

Penguins are flightless birds, but they are excellent swimmers. **Emperor penguins** can swim faster than 18.5 miles (30 kilometers) per hour.

Fairy penguins are the smallest penguins. They grow to about 17 inches (43 centimeters) tall.

Ostriches are the largest and fastest land bird. They can reach 9 feet (2.7 meters) tall and can run at speeds of up to 40 miles (65 kilometers) per hour. However, they cannot fly.

Emus come from Australia. They are related to ostriches. Emu chicks have brown and cream stripes to help them hide.

Emu eggs are dark green. The female lays up to 15 eggs in a nest. Then the male sits on the eggs for 55 days without drinking, eating, or leaving the nest.

Rheas live in South America. Males raise newborn chicks alone for the first six months. They protect their chicks by kicking at predators.

Like ducks, **grebes** can swim and dive well, but they walk clumsily. Some species are reluctant to fly, while two species in South America are completely flightless.

Kiwis are native to New Zealand. They are the only birds with nostrils at the end of their bill. They sleep during the day and feed at night.

New Zealand **kakapos** are the only parrots that cannot fly. However, they are good climbers. There are fewer than 100 kakapos left in the world.

Flying Bugs

Flying insects help spread seeds and pollen so that plants can reproduce. They are the only animals with no backbone that have developed wings to fly.

Some **butterflies** have brightly-colored wings to scare away predators. Some patterns help to hide butterflies in their surroundings.

Butterflies hold their wings vertically when resting. They also have thin feelers, or antennae.

Moths hold their wings horizontally when resting. They have feathery antennae.

Dragonflies can fly up to 30 miles (50 kilometers) per hour. They can also fly backward, hover in the air, and zigzag quickly.

Male **cicadas** are the loudest insects. They sing by vibrating thin membranes at the base of their abdomen.

Grasshoppers chirp by rubbing their hind legs against their wings. A grasshopper can leap 20 times the length of its own body.

Lacewings have two sets of lace-like wings. Adult lacewings lay eggs that hatch into larvae. Larvae then eat aphids and caterpillars.

Honeybees gather nectar from flowers. They mix nectar and pollen, and store it on their legs.

Ladybugs have spotted front wings. To fly, they open their front wings and unfold their back wings.